Thoughts Running Around My Head

Amy Liao

BookLeaf
Publishing

India | USA | UK

Presentation by *BookLeaf Publishing*

Web: www.bookleafpub.com

E-mail: info@bookleafpub.com

ISBN: 978-93-5744-725-6

First edition 2022

DEDICATION

Dedicated to Shuren Liao and Shan Li

ACKNOWLEDGEMENT

I would like to thank my extraordinary parents, Shuren Liao and Shan Li, for always letting my imagination run wild. Also, special thanks to all of my English teachers over the years who have inspired my love for writing.

Restaurant Thoughts

The waiter leaves the table with the menus
And anticipation fills everyone's mind
Their stomachs are rumbling like wheels on
pavement
Their eyes are darting towards their watch
Waiting to see when their food will arrive
Somewhere in the restaurant's kitchen
A cook is sizzling, frying, grilling, baking
Perhaps a cook is cooking their order right now
The wait is unbearable
Their stomachs grow impatient
But wait-
The waiter comes back
Like a circus act, juggling many plates at once
Just by looking at the food
Everyone's stomach has been reassured
It's time to eat.

Trapped

Imagine staying in one place
For your entire existence on Earth
That is essentially my life
For I am a fish who lives in a tank.

No matter how much I swim
I can never get anywhere
This tank is all I've ever known
And all I will ever experience.

Embroiled in this prison
Confined forever and ever
Surrounded by glass my entire life
I can go no farther than that.

I envy the fish in the sea
Who have no owners
Who have no boundaries
Who are truly free.

I am a fish who lives in a tank
This tank makes me feel imprisoned
Like it is limiting my curiosity
Like I am trapped in my own life.

Subway People

I get on the subway at Huntingdon station
Like I do every day to go to school
I sit at my favorite seat next to the door
Ready to see the most interesting of things:

A businesswoman sits across from me
Her suit nicely steamed, her suitcase by her side
She looks so professional and intimidating
As she vigorously texts while scrunching her
eyebrows.

A homeless man sits a few seats away from her
Sleeping peacefully as if everything was perfect
His leg is bandaged, his skin covered in dirt
I can´t help but wonder what his story is.

A student sits two seats away from me
Like me, his backpack is stuffed to the brim
I watch as he chaotically scribbles in a notebook
with a pen
He must have forgotten to do his homework.

I stare at these people on the subway
Curious about their lives
I think about them until I realize-
It´s time to get off at my stop.

The Pool

My body shivers
As I stand over the pool
My goggles over my eyes
My swim cap, uncomfortably tight

I jump into the pool
And with a loud splash
I wince as I hit the water
I get a cold, icy shock

I rise above the water
And despite the coldness
I savor the moment
In which I first touch the pool
My skin embracing it all.

Chips

Avocados, zucchini, and baloney,
Carrots, apples, and macaroni,
Cheese, crackers, and layered taco dip,
So many foods, yet I only want is chips,
Chips: the salty goodness,
Each bag filled with irresistible crunchiness,
Something so cheap, but brings me so much glee,
I savor every bite of this delicious beauty,
Chips give me so much bliss,
Despite my health teacher's dismissiveness,
Chips always satisfy my cravings,
I will buy them until I have no more savings,
Found in the snack aisle of the grocery store,
Chips are something that I will always be in need of more.

The Present Moment

We can't change the past
Whatever mistakes we made
Regrets we have
Are now set in stone

We can't predict the future
How many kids we will have
Or how much money we will make
The future is an unforeseeable unknown

Yet we are living in the present
So we should be in the moment
Stop dwelling on the past
And worrying about the future
Cherish what is called "now".

Testing

Tick tock, tick tock,
Time is running out
There is almost no time left
On the steadily ticking clock

I run through all the questions
On this nerve-wracking test
Not confident in any of my answers
I should have studied more than I had

We are all so focused, no one makes a peep
"Time's up!" the teacher says all of sudden
Scared and panicked by these words,
I lower my head and weep.

Gray Skys

I watch as raindrops fall from the sky
Like tears running down someone's face
And the sky itself- gray and depressing
There is little change in the weather

I feel trapped in this dull and solemn sky
It makes me feel unmotivated and sad
Like there is nothing good to come
This is the weather every single day

I long for the day that spring arrives
Where flowers bloom and the trees grow green
Where the blue sky and sun finally awaken
But until then, the gray sky and rain will stay.

The "Perfect" Life

A long row of big houses
That look exactly the same
In the middle of the suburbs
Each has a big grass lawn
And boys and girls playing
On the perfectly paved sidewalk

The dads cook barbeques
And watch sports games
The moms gossip at book club
And start a vegetable garden

In the humongous backyard
There are swing sets and picnic tables
Pools and perfectly cut grass
While the family dog happily runs around

The spitting image of the perfect life
Of the American dream
That is everyday life for some
But far from reality for others.

A Funny Thing Called Time

Time- it's a funny thing
Something that seems so slow
When in the very moment
Yet feels so fast as a whole

One minute, we are young children
Innocent, curious about everything
The next minute, we are grown
Knowing more about the world

Time is a fever dream
It doesn't feel like much
Until we look back and think
Where has it all gone?

Costco

There are many stores across the world
Clothing shops and fast-food restaurants
Grocery stores and city bodegas
But the only store that matters to me
Is the one and only… Costco!

Costco, Costco, how to begin?
Their free samples are always tasty
Delicious, scrumptious, and satisfies my
cravings
An iconic part of Costco's store.

Then there are the humongous amounts
Of food, drinks, books, clothes, school supplies
You name it, this warehouse has got it in bulk
And for a surprisingly low price.

The food court is always a fun place to stop by
After an hour-long shopping trip
With their famously cheap hot dogs
And long, sweet churros with cinnamon.

Costco: always my number one weekend
destination
Whether it's to get my week's supply of food

Or simply just to browse around
Costco will forever be my favorite place to go.

12

It All Seemed So Simple

It all seemed so simple
When I was a baby
And all I could do
Was lay around all-day
And be engulfed with my own curiosity.

It all seemed so simple
When I was a kid
Running around happily
Playing to my heart's desire
With not a single care in the world.

It all seemed so simple
When I was a teenager
Going to school every day
Not having to worry about money
Always sure that my parents were there
To cook a meal for me.

It all seemed so simple at the time,
But in reality, life is hard at any stage of life
No matter where you are or what time it is
You just have to keep on pushing through.

Mornings

The sky is still dark
A long day of school awaits
I hate the mornings.

The Spicy Chicken Wing

Nervous and afraid, yet willing to try
I bite into the blazing burst of heat
That is the spicy chicken wing
Sitting on my otherwise empty plate

Made from a mean ghost pepper sauce
This chicken wing is more than just food,
It's hot enough to be the whole sun-
I breathe in and out, in and out
Not being able to handle it anymore

The feeling takes over my body
My mouth feels like it is on fire
And so I run over to the fridge
To pour me a tall cold glass of milk
Where I can finally relieve myself.

It Only Takes One

I walk down the stairs at school
Carrying a mountain load of books
Wobbling dangerously each time I take a step
As if I were a circus act trying to balance plates
Then all of a sudden- SMASH!
All my books topple over to the ground
So feeling my face turn red with embarrassment
From the dozens of people staring at me
And walking past as I scramble to get my things
I quickly try to grab all my books into a pile
Until one person, quiet and shy
Reaches down to help me stack my books
It only takes one.

Precious Time

1,440 minutes
86,400 seconds
And 24 hours in a day-
Yet I still feel like
There isn't enough time
To do what I need to do
To say what I have to say
To enjoy what I want to enjoy
Oh, how I wish
I could wave a magic wand
And all of a sudden
I have all the time in the world
But sadly, that doesn't exist
We all just have to make the best
And cherish our precious time.

What Makes a Hero?

What makes a hero?
Do they have to fly like Peter Pan
Or be as strong as Hercules?
No, anybody can be a hero
Even if they are just regular people

Does a hero have to wear a cape?
Or be in good shape?
No, anybody can be a hero
Even a random person on the street

A hero is courageous and compassionate
And will sacrifice themselves for others
A true hero does not wear a cape
It is their actions that make them heroic

A hero could be anyone:
A classmate,
A neighbor,
A fireman,
Being a hero isn't all about saving people from
evil villains
Everyone has the capability of being a hero.

Procrastinator

Let's all be honest here:
We've all been a procrastinator
At one point in our lives
Whether it be not studying for a test
Or responding to an email
We've all been there.
That stressed feeling we get
When we wait until the last minute
Putting off whatever we have to do
The only thing motivating us
Is the due date of the homework
Or the deadline of the work application
But sometimes we have to remember
That life has a deadline too
Life is short-
So we shouldn't procrastinate
What we've been meaning to do.

Chilly Winter Mornings

As I step out the door to go to school
A chilly gust of wind hits my face
Although I am wearing four layers
I am still welcomed with a cold embrace

Oh, the winter mornings-
Where the sky is still dark out
And the sun hasn't even woken up yet
I'm too sleepy to even pout

How I long to be in my cozy bed
Where my blanket cuddles me
And I get to sleep in peace
Away in my dreams where I am free.

The Power of Music

Music is so many things
To so many people
And the power it holds is magical:

Music is the universal language
That brings everyone together
And shines some light into our world
Even people in the darkest of times

Music is the difficult frustration
When I am practicing my flute
Yet, despite what a challenge it is
I am still grateful for the gift
Of being able to play music

Music is so common in our lives
Something that has such a great impact
Yet we all still take it for granted
Imagine a world without music?
What a sad world that would be.

Life is a Treat

Life is full of twists and turns
Just like frozen yogurt
On a hot summer's day

There are the high points in life
The very best moments
The times we cherish most

There are low points in life
Our bad days and worst memories
Our deepest fears come to be true

But every day is still a gift
Just like frozen yogurt
That's why it's called a treat.

www.ingramcontent.com/pod-product-compliance
Lightning Source LLC
LaVergne TN
LVHW050506210726

843509LV00015BA/3021